Legends of Country Music

George Jones

An unauthorized fan tribute

By: James Hoag

Paperback Edition

Manufactured in the United States of America

TABLE OF CONTENTS

INTRODUCTION

I write this in May of 2013. It's only been a couple weeks since George Jones passed away. I am still in mourning. He was, in my opinion and in the opinion of many others, the greatest country singer in the history of country music. He started back in the day when country was called hillbilly and he was still going strong last year in 2012.

Back in 2005, I think it was, George came to Wendover, Nevada which is near where I live and my wife and I had the opportunity to see him in person. What a night. We came home singing all the great songs.

My favorite of George's is "He Stopped Loving Her Today" which is probably everyone's favorite. Some say this song is the greatest country song ever written,

When the New York Times wrote up the details of his death in April, 2013, the headline read, "His Life was a Country Song". I can think of no line that better describes George Jones. He was one of my heroes and I hope he was one of yours.

Waylon Jennings, another great country singer and possibly the subject of a future "Legends of Country Music" book said in his song "It's Alright" which came out on his album "Music Man' in 1980, said this in the song "If we all could sound like we wanted to, we'd all sound like George Jones." I think that about sums it up.

(Author's Note: All references in this book to "charts" refer to the Billboard Country Charts, either singles or albums, unless otherwise indicated.)

GROWING UP IN TEXAS

Like most country singers, George Jones was born and raised in the south. That is, if you consider Texas to be part of the south. Personally, I think Texas is west, not south, but that's probably a matter of opinion.

George was born George Glenn Jones in Saratoga, Texas on September 12, 1931 in a log cabin. It's reported in most places I read that he came out of his mother with a broken arm. According to George, he was a heavy baby, over eight pounds and when the doctor took hold of him for the first time, he dropped him, breaking his arm. So George started out life with trauma. Saratoga is about 40 miles northwest of Beaumont, Texas and about 75 miles northeast of Houston. It is in the heart of the Texas oil fields. His parents were Clare and George Washington Jones. His father, also George, was a truck driver, a pipe-fitter and a moonshiner.

When George was young, the family moved to Vidor, Texas. Vidor is just outside of Beaumont. George had one brother and five sisters when he was born. He would have had one more sister, Ethel but she died seven years before George was born. That was when Daddy took up drinking.

George, like most boys in east Texas, in the Thirties and Forties enjoyed country and gospel music. His family had accumulated a number of Carter Family records and George listened to them over and over. He got his gospel training, like so many others, going to church with his family. He liked to listen to the radio and country music was about all you get on the dial in those days and in that part of the country. So, George listened to country music. When he was seven, his father bought him a guitar and that was the beginning of a career. With the help of his Sunday School teacher, he began to learn chords. The family was poor; this was the depression, after all. With his father's help, George found that he could earn pennies if he stood on a street corner and play that guitar and sing. He would also play in church every chance he got and performed on the local radio station. Everyone thought he was so cute.

Today, Interstate 10 goes right by Vidor, Texas. In 1968, I drove Interstate 10 from New Orleans to Utah. I must have passed right by George Jones's house. If I had known then what I know now, I would have stopped and taken a look around. In 1968, I really didn't know country music existed.

George started out at about the age of fourteen, playing for a local Beaumont couple named Eddie and Pearl. They were married and played country music live on a morning radio show in Beaumont. George got in with them and managed to get them to agree to let him play. At first, he didn't sing, just played, but eventually they found out that he could sing and so, they included him in the songs. It was Eddie who named him "The Possum", a name that would stick with him for the rest of his life. Eddie named him that because, he said, George's eyes were close together and his nose turned up, sort of like a possum.

George liked playing the guitar and singing for people, but wanted to do it on his own. So, in 1945, he ran away from home and traveled to Jasper, Texas which is a little more than 60 miles north of Vidor, leaving his family behind. Upon arriving in Jasper, he got together with a local musician, Dalton Henderson, who also played country music and the two of them started singing together. George says the first time he ever got drunk was with Dalton Henderson. They got a job playing and singing on a local radio station, KTXJ, in Jasper. Today, the station plays gospel music to all of eastern Texas and western Louisiana.

MARRIAGE NUMBER ONE

George Jones was destined to marry four times in his life. He only held on to the last one, Nancy, who was at his side when he died.

His first marriage was to Dorothy Bonvillion in 1950 when he was 17. George's mother had to sign the papers allowing him to get married since he was underage. George was broke, essentially, and they had no place to live, so they moved in with Dorothy's parents. This is a bad way to start a marriage, especially if the husband is gone all the time playing music and getting drunk. Dorothy's father attempted to hire George as a house painter, but George wouldn't stick with it.

As expected, the marriage didn't last long; after just over a year, they split up and were divorced. He left even before their daughter, Susan, was born. The breakup was blamed on George's drinking which had already started, but it was probably more than that. I suspect Dorothy's parents had a lot to do with it. I can't imagine what happened in the Jones household, but George couldn't pay child support because he was literally broke most of the time. Dorothy had him arrested and he spent five days in jail. Upon getting out, the court ordered him to pay child support and since he really couldn't afford it, he joined the Marines so he would have a salary to send home.

Although this was right in the middle of the Korean War, George did not see combat while he was in the Marines. In fact, he found many opportunities to sing in local clubs where ever he was stationed and continued to improve on his craft. He was in the Marines from 1950 until 1953. It was during his time in the Marines that he heard the news that he said affected him for a long time. "Hank Williams is dead". Hank Williams was killed in an automobile accident on his way to a concert. Williams was one of three country music idols that influenced everything George did. The other two were Roy Acuff and Lefty

Frizzell. George said he laid in his bunk and bawled when he heard that Hank Williams had been killed.

After three years in the Marines, he got out and still needing a job; became a disc jockey for radio station KTRM in Beaumont, Texas. KTRM was just a small AM-station that broadcast country and rock and roll. J.P. Richardson, who later became known as The Big Bopper (and died in the famous airplane crash with Buddy Holly in 1959), got his start as a disc jockey at KTRM. Today, the station doesn't exist as an AM-station, but the call letters have been resurrected and now belong to Truman State University in Kirksville, Missouri.

STARDAY RECORDS

George, still following his dream of performing, got jobs singing in the local clubs in and around Beaumont. Two record producers happened to catch him one night and decided they liked what they heard. Jack Stames and Harold W. Daily (better known as "Pappy") owned Starday Records. Starday is a combination of their two names. Although they were headquartered in Beaumont, they were a major record company for the time period (at least in the state of Texas) and became even greater after hiring George Jones.

He signed a recording contract and the first record he recorded was called "No Money in This Deal". The record was recorded in the living room of Jack Stames and, in those days, everything was done in one take. There were no tracks. If someone in the band made a mistake, it either went out like that or they started over and did it again. Stames tacked egg cartons on the walls to control the sound as it was being recorded.

Pappy listened to George sing and after a few minutes, stopped him. He told George, you sound like Lefty Frizzell or Hank Williams or Roy Acuff. George told him that they were his heroes and he wanted to sound like them. Pappy said the world already had a Hank Williams, it didn't need another one. He wanted to hear what George Jones sounded like. And so, George began to develop the distinctive George Jones style that we love so much today.

There are just a couple copies of "No Money in This Deal" on YouTube and I'm not sure if they are the original or not, but it is a fun song that has all the elements of early country music. It didn't make an impact on anyone and if you check out discographies on the internet, it's not even mentioned. It's a good song and I won't forget it, so it's included in the list of singles George had at the end of this book.

Other records followed which are probably pretty valuable today. Songs like "Play It Cool, Man", "Let Him Know" and "You All Goodnight". In all, he recorded six records or twelve sides in 1954 and none of them did much of anything. Then in 1955, he found the right song.

MARRIAGE NUMBER TWO

In 1954, George was busy trying to break into Country Music in a big way when he happened to stop in Houston at a local drive-in. There was a car-hop working there taking orders and delivering food and he couldn't take his eyes off her.

Her name was Shirley Corey and George decided he needed to meet her. So, he started flirting with her and they dated and on September 14, 1954, she became Mrs. George Jones. This would be wife number two for George. This marriage lasted longer than the first one and he and Shirley had two children together, Jeffrey and Brian. They were married for fourteen years, but Shirley's heart was never really in it. She didn't like what George did for a living and sometimes George would come home from a trip out of town to play a show and she would just be gone.

It's probably surprising that the marriage lasted as long as it did.

The first hit George had with Starday was "Why Baby Why" and that one is mentioned on all the lists. The song reached number four on the country charts and the original record is reported to be worth about $50 today. "Why Baby Why" was co-written by George and was his breakthrough hit, but in those days, more than one artist would often record a song. There were several versions of "Why Baby Why" over the years, but in 1955, Webb Pierce and Red Sovine did a cover of the song and since they were well know and no one had heard of George yet, their version went right to number one and George was drowned out. But that didn't stop him.

George wanted to get to the ultimate place in Country Music in those days (still is), The Grand Ole Opry, but he couldn't get an invitation. So, he played for the Louisiana Hayride, a show that often proved to be a stepping stone to the Opry. George recounts the first time he played at the Hayride, there was this shy boy who kept to himself and stayed in his dressing room a lot. He was promoting a new kind of music that was just emerging in the United States. It was called rock and roll. The boy? Elvis Presley.

He continued to put out records. Next was "What Am I Worth" (#7), "You Gotta Be My Baby" (#7), "Just One More" (#3), "Yearning" (#10) and a few others you can check out in the Selected Discography section. Rock and Roll was becoming really big. In fact, it was overtaking country as the favorite music in the South and country labels were concerned. So Pappy convinced George to write and record two rock and roll songs. They released the record under the name of Thumper Jones. The name is literally taken from the character of Thumper in the Bambi movie. There are some people today who believe this was not George, but I've listened to the record and I believe it is him. George himself says it's him. The record was called "Rock It"/"How Come It" and is pure rockabilly. Quite different from the country for which he became known. The record sank without much notice, but today an original record is worth between $250 and $500. Wish I had one. Both songs can be heard on YouTube, of course.

In August of 1956, George finally got his wish and got the call to come play at The Grand Ole Opry which was broadcast from Nashville, Tennessee. By the end of the year, he had released his first album, called "Grand Ole Opry's New Star". It contained three of the hits he had had up to this point starting with "Why Baby Why". George either wrote or co-wrote all of the songs on the album. This was Starday's very first album as a company. It put both George and the company on a firm financial footing for the future.

In 1957, Starday signed an agreement with Mercury Records to release George's work under that label. Pappy Daily still kept control of his contract, but George would now have a much broader distribution and could get his music in front of more people. The first record he released for Mercury was "Don't Stop the Music" which reached number 10 on the charts.

In mid-1957, he recorded "Too Much Water" which peaked at number 13. This song was written by George and Sonny James. Sonny James was a rising young star in Country music, himself, having had a gigantic number one hit the year before with "Young Love" which crossed over to the pop charts.

"WHITE LIGHTNING"

In 1959, George hit pay dirt. "White Lightning" was George's first number one song. It was written by his old friend from the radio station, J.P. Richardson. The song spent five weeks at number one.

I mentioned before that Richardson died with Buddy Holly in the famous plane crash of February, 1959. It was just two months later in April that "White Lightning" hit number one. Richardson did not get to see it. "White Lightning" was difficult to record because George was already establishing his reputation as a drinker. George would show up at the studio drunk and then attempt to record. It took over 80 takes before they got a good recording. His bass player, Buddy Killen threatened to quit the recording because he had blisters on his fingers from playing the same parts over and over 80 times.

Thus began the legend that would follow George most of the rest of his life. George and alcohol were good friends. Despite the drinking, George managed to put out the hits. In 1959 he charted with "Who Shot Sam" (#7) and "Money to Burn" (#15).

By the end of the Fifties, he had released five albums, three on the Starday label and two on Mercury. "Grand Ole Opry's New Star" was in 1957, "Hillbilly Hit Parade" and "Long Live King George" in 1958 and "Country Church Time" and "White Lightning and Other Favorites" in 1959. He was just getting started.

The Sixties came in with a bang. After a couple lesser hits, he recorded "The Window Up Above" which made it to number two. Mickey Gilley would record the song in 1975 and get a number one. The song was written by George, however. Then, in 1961, he had his second number one song with "Tender Years" which was written by Darrell Edwards and George stayed at the top for seven weeks. In a rare happening, this song actually made the Billboard Hot 100 pop charts where it peaked at number 76.

His next hit was "Aching Breaking Heart" which reached number five in 1962. (Not to be confused with "Achy Breaky Heart" by Billy Ray Cyrus in 1992.) This would be his last hit on the Mercury label as he moved over to the United Artists label. George started his career at United Artists with a song that would become a standard for George. "She Thinks I Still Care" became his third number one song, staying at the top for six weeks. The song was written by Dickey Lee and Steve Duffy. The flip side "Sometimes You Just Can't Win" reached number 17 on the charts. Unfortunately, this would be his last number one for five years.

Connie Francis covered the song in 1962 as "He Thinks I Still Care", but she failed to make the Top 40 with the song, only reaching number 57. The song has since been recorded by several people, like Anne Murray and even Elvis Presley.

MELBA MONTGOMERY

In 1963, George had a major career shift in that he got together with another rising star in Nashville, Melba Montgomery. Montgomery was a singer and a song writer just like George and she had written a song called "We Must Have Been Out of Our Minds". Duets have always been a staple of country music and this was not the first time George would team up with someone else, but, so far, it was the most successful. He teamed up with country singer Margie Singleton for "Did I Ever Tell You" (#15) in 1961 and again for "Waltz of the Angels" (#11) in 1962.

Montgomery had done several solo records, but had not had a hit yet. At the time she was recording for the United Artists label as was George. The two got together, recorded the duet and magic happened. "We Must Have Been Out of Our Minds" reached number three on the charts and stayed on Billboard's Country Chart for 33 weeks that year.

George would continue to record with Montgomery and they would have hits off and on until 1967. But "We Must Have Been Out of Our Minds" would be their only Top 10 song. George, even though married, was very smitten with Montgomery. Many times he tried to get her to go out with him. They were on the road, far from home, who would know? But Montgomery avoided his advances and eventually married another man, so George never got the chance to cheat.

Country music was changing in the Sixties. It was becoming a little more mainstream and the artists looked less and less like cowboys and more and more like regular performers. None of that bothered George. He was never really a cowboy, but he loved to dress up in the sparkle and spangle of the day. His suits were covered with sequins and he did wear cowboy boots, although I haven't seen many pictures of him wearing a cowboy hat or any kind of hat at all. If you look at all of the pictures on the first page of Google (after entering George Jones and selecting images), there is only one picture with him wearing a hat and that was taken when he was very young.

In 1964, George had a couple Top 10 songs with "Your Heart Turned Left (When I Was on the Right)" (#5) and "Where Does a Little Tear Come From" (#10) when he got all the way to number three with "The Race Is On" written by Don Rollins. The song originated with George, but was covered in 1965 by Jack Jones (no relation) where it reached number 15 on the Billboard Top 40 charts. The song has been covered by lots of others including an unlikely Grateful Dead. Later in 1989, the country group Sawyer Brown did their version of the song.

George was no longer recording for Starday, having left them years before, but he was still associated with Pappy Daily who had become his manager. Under Daily's guidance, George moved to Musicor Records in 1965 and began a career with them that would last until 1971. The first single he did for Musicor was "Things Have Gone to Pieces" which reached number nine on the charts. His first album for the label was "Mr. Country and Western Music" which peaked at number 13 on the Country Albums chart.

During his stay with Musicor, he recorded over 300 songs for them. Of those, 17 made the Top 10. "Love Bug" has become something of a country classic over the years. George reached number six with the song and then in 1994, George Strait did a version of the song which reached number eight. It's a fun song about getting bitten by the "love bug". I think most of us have had that pleasure.

GEORGE JONES AND GENE PITNEY

In 1965, after joining Musicor, he joined up with Gene Pitney. Now, if you were alive in the Sixties and listened to the radio at all, you probably remember Gene Pitney, even if you didn't listen to country music. Pitney would have sixteen Top 40 pop hits during the Sixties, starting in 1961 and running through 1968. The biggest hit he had was the number two song "Only Love Can Break a Heart". I can hear it in my head right now.

Pitney joined up with George in 1965 and their first hit was "I've Got Five Dollars and It's Saturday Night", a fun, pure country song that will have your toes tapping. The song peaked at number sixteen for them. They went on to hit the charts three more times, "Louisiana Man" (#25), "Big Job" (#50) and "That's All It Took" (#47)

Next was George's fourth number one song. He hadn't recorded a number one since 1962 and it was a long dry spell even though he had been recording and charting right along. "Walk Through This World With Me" was written by Sandy Seamond and Kaye Savage. It's a beautiful love song about a man proclaiming his love for his woman and asking her to always be by his side. It stayed at number one for two weeks and was on the charts a total of 19 weeks. That same year, 1967, Engelbert Humperdinck recorded a pop version of the song. The song was included on Humperdinck's first album "Release Me", but was never released as a single and, therefore, didn't chart.

Also, we have "If My Heart Had Windows" which George released in 1967 and peaked at number seven. It was written by Dallas Frazier who has written many country songs and a few pop ones as well. Remember "Alley Oop", recorded by the Hollywood Argyles in 1960? Frazier wrote that. Another song I like which was recorded by Frazier himself in 1966 called "Elvira" was made famous when the

Oak Ridge Boys recorded it in 1981 and it was number one on the country charts and number five on the pop charts.

THE LEGEND OF THE LAWN MOWER

George was going deeper into the bottle every day. There is a story which some believe is an urban myth, but, I'm pretty sure, did happen. Shirley would have to leave the house occasionally to go shopping or something, so to keep George home and out of the bars, she would hide the keys to the cars that they owned.

One night, George woke up and wanted to go to town to the nearest tavern in Beaumont, but it was eight miles away and Shirley had hid his keys. He couldn't find them anywhere. Then he remembered the lawn mower in the garage. He got on the riding lawn mower and at about 5 miles an hour, made the trip into town. It took an hour and a half to make the journey. When Shirley came home, she found George gone and knew right where he was. They say George just laughed when Shirley came through the door of the tavern.

Believe it or not, this incident was repeated years later when he was married to Tammy Wynette. Tammy reports that she woke up at 1 a.m. one night and found George gone. She got dressed and drove to the nearest tavern and, sure enough, right in from of the tavern sat their green John Deere lawn mower. As she entered the tavern, George looked up and told his friends, "There's the little woman. I told you she would come for me."

This incident has been embellished and made fun of for years. There are at least three country videos which feature George riding a lawn tractor. George himself made fun of it in the song "Honky Tonk Song" in 1996 which only peaked at number 66 on the charts, but it relates a story of a cop pulling him over and walking up to him, he says "Get off that riding mower" George explains, "She took my keys and now she won't drive me to drink". It's a cute George Jones song. I'm surprised it didn't do better, but this was the Nineties and people weren't listening to Honky Tonk much anymore.

In 1984, Hank Williams Jr. recorded a video for "All My Rowdy Friends Are Coming Over Tonight" which played on CMT and MTV. As the guests are arriving, there is quick flash of George riding his lawn mower to the party. Vince Gill did "One More Last Chance" in 1993 about a wife who wouldn't let him go to the tavern. With a nod to George Jones, Gill sings, "Well she might've took my car keys, But she forgot about my old John Deere" The video takes place pretty much at a golf course and at the end, as Gill is leaving on his tractor, he passes George on his lawn mower. He calls "Hey Possum" as they pass. George replies "Hey Sweet Pea", which was George's nickname for Gill. A third video is John Rich's "Country Done Come to Town", from 2010, shows George mowing the grass on the patio of a building, riding his mower. All three videos are available on YouTube.

In 1968, his second wife, Shirley had had enough of his shenanigans and filed for divorce. George just kept drinking. It didn't take long George to bounce back, at least in the love department. He moved to Nashville where he met what was then, the First Lady of Country Music, Tammy Wynette. They started seeing each other and soon fell in love. George and Tammy got married on February 16, 1969, less than a year after his divorce from Shirley. They would be called Country Royalty, since George was the King of Country Music (at least in a lot of people's eyes) and Tammy was the First Lady. Now they were married. It was a perfect union in most people's eyes. It was as big as or bigger than the union of Johnny Cash and June Carter.

MARRIAGE NUMBER THREE - TAMMY WYNETTE

Let's take a short break from George and talk about the most important partner he had, at least as far as music is concerned, Tammy Wynette.

Tammy Wynette was born Virginia Wynette Pugh on May 5, 1942. She was the only child of William Hollis Pugh, who passed away before she even turned one on February 13, 1943, and Mildred Faye Russell who became a single mother with a baby girl at the age of twenty.

Tammy was born and raised near the tiny town of Tremont, Mississippi. Tremont is on the eastern edge of Mississippi just a few miles from Alabama. In 2000, it had a population of 350, so in 1942, I imagine it was much less than that. Tammy's mother Mildred didn't want to have to take care of a daughter without a husband, so she dropped Tammy off with her parents and moved to Memphis to work for the war effort. Tammy grew up on a farm with her grandparents and her aunt Carolyn. She spent much of her childhood working the fields and picking cotton.

Her mother remarried in 1946, but to my knowledge, never came back to get Tammy. You've probably seen Tammy on television or in videos, so you know she was a tall woman. It's not surprising that she was a star basketball player in high school. She, like so many in the south, longed to be a country singer.

Just before graduating high school, she married her first husband, Euple Byrd. The problem was that Byrd didn't share her vision of being a singer. He thought it was nonsense. So, Tammy ended up doing what most young wives did in Mississippi with only a high school education. She waited tables, did some bartending, worked as a receptionist and any other job she could get.

In 1963, she went to beauty school in Tupelo, Mississippi and became a hairdresser. Fortunately for us, she didn't have to work as a hair dresser for very long, but she did renew her license every year in case she needed another career to fall back on. After two kids and still no moral support from her husband, she decided to cut him loose and carrying their third child still unborn, she left Byrd and moved to Birmingham, Alabama.

In Birmingham, she got a night job singing for a local television station, WBRC-TV on the Country Boy Eddie Show. This was 1965. It was through her job on WBRC that she met Porter Wagoner and decided to move to Nashville with her three children. She tried almost every recording studio in town and was rejected by them all. Then she met Billy Sherrill who was a producer for Epic Records. He just happened to need a singer for a new song called "Apartment No 9". The song was written by Johnny Paycheck, but they really needed a woman to sing the lyrics as the song seems to be from the woman's point of view. Tammy was in the right place at the right time and Billy Sherrill liked her for the spot. He signed her to Epic Records.

So, "Apartment No 9" was Tammy's first hit even if it only got to number 44 on the country charts. She was on her way and only a year later would have a number one with "My Elusive Dreams", a duet she did with David Houston.

She was still Virginia Pugh Byrd at this time and Sherrill wanted her to change her name to something a little more country, I guess. When she first met Sherrill, she had her hair up in a ponytail and that blonde ponytail reminded Sherrill of Debbie Reynolds who played in the movie "Tammy and the Bachelor", a big movie during the Fifties. He told her, from now on you will be known as Tammy and since her last name stinks, she became just Tammy Wynette using her middle name as a last name.

She followed up "Apartment No. 9" with "Your Good Girl's Gonna Go Bad" which peaked at number 3. Not everyone can hit a home run only the second time up to bat, but Tammy did. She went on to hit number one with "I Don't Wanna Play House", a song written by her mentor, Billy Sherrill and Glenn Sutton. They called Tammy Wynette the "First Lady of Country Music" and it could be because she just kept hitting number one. She would go on to have 20 number ones in her career, several, of course, with George Jones. But before she met and married George, she had five number ones on her own. One of which would prove to be a little prophetic, "D-I-V-O-R-C-E". The song stayed at the top for three weeks and if Tammy wasn't a superstar before she recorded that song, she certainly was afterwards.

Another song which Tammy actually recorded before she married George was "Stand By Your Man". Both songs seem prophetic now after knowing what we know of their tumultuous relationship and marriage and breakup. "Stand By Your Man" has gone on to become a country classic in every sense of the word. It is one of the most covered country songs in history. It was also the only song that crossed over to the pop charts by Tammy Wynette where it reached number nineteen.

THE KING AND FIRST LADY OF COUNTRY MUSIC

Since George and Tammy were now married, they naturally wanted to sing together. But there was one big problem. George recorded on Musicor and Tammy recorded on Epic labels. Epic wouldn't let Tammy record on Musicor and vice versa. The only solution was for both of them to get on the same label.

George was growing more and more unhappy with Pappy Daily who produced him on Musicor. He was not getting the number one hits anymore and he didn't like the sound that he was recording. He blamed all of that on Daily. So, George proceeded to try to get out of his contract. It wasn't easy, but by the end of 1971, he had fulfilled his contract with Musicor and severed ties with them. To do so, however, he had to give up rights to all the music he had recorded for Musicor. He didn't care, he wanted out, no matter what the cost. He immediately signed with Epic and would stay with Epic for most of the rest of his career.

Changing labels had the immediate effect of allowing him and Tammy to perform and record together. Their first record together was "Take Me" which George had done solo back in 1965 and which peaked at number eight on the charts. The new version included both of them singing together and peaked at number nine, just one spot below George's version.

Billy Sherrill, who had been Tammy's producer for several years, also became George's producer. His work ethic was quite different from Pappy Daily and, at first, the two didn't get along. George was used to a calm relaxed atmosphere when he recorded and Sherrill was somewhat of a taskmaster. Everything had to done exactly to his specifications. George didn't like this at first, but gradually grew to accept it and even like it.

George's previous music had been more of a "Honky Tonk" style. The sort of music you heard in the bar when you were drunk. Now, Sherrill molded him into being a more mainstream country singer, a balladeer. Most of his work for Epic for the next twenty years would be more of the love song variety instead of the saloon variety. It was said that Sherrill sanded off the rough edges of George Jones.

His first solo for Epic was a nod to his new wife and their relationship. "We Can Make It" reached number six in February of 1972. He followed that up with the number two "Loving You Could Never Be Better". Then he and Tammy recorded their second duet together "The Ceremony" which would go to number six in the United States. The songs portrays a wedding ceremony where a voice in the background (the minister) asks each of them if they will love, honor and obey each other for the rest of their lives. Then Tammy sings her vows and George sings his vows and it feels like you are right there at the wedding. Too bad they didn't listen to the vows themselves.

TROUBLE IN PARADISE

But, as close as they seemed when they sang their songs, there was trouble in paradise. By now, George was deep into alcohol and drugs. And he really didn't care who knew it. He and Tammy began to fight, offstage, of course. To the public, George and Tammy seemed to be the perfect couple, but gradually even they began to see the cracks in the marriage.

They sang love songs on stage. George continued to release records. Some did well and some not so well. One of the successful ones was "A Picture of Me (Without You)" which peaked at number five in October of 1972. A mournful song that sounds like lost love to me. Can you imagine a sky without blue, a garden where nothing is growing or a world where there is no music, then that's the way I feel without you. This song is very similar to an old Webb Pierce song called "That's Me Without You" which came out in 1953.

After a couple of mediocre hits in 1973, "Old Fashioned Singing" (#38) and "Let's Build a World Together" (#32), George and Tammy hit gold again with the number one song "We're Gonna Hold On". It's another love song which sounds like they will be together forever. Watching the videos of this song, you can see the love in the eyes of both of them. I suspect if George could have controlled his demons, they might have stayed together.

Just before "We're Gonna Hold On" came out, Tammy actually filed for divorce in August, 1973, but she reconsidered and withdrew the petition and things went on. Listening to the song makes you wonder if maybe they are going to keep their marriage together. But, it was not to be, George was slowly killing himself with alcohol and drugs.

THE END OF THE ROYAL MARRIAGE

1974 was a good year for George, but it would his last good year for quite a while. He had his fifth solo number one song with "The Grand Tour". This was also the title track to the album he released in 1974. The song has been called a perfect country song. Since divorce is one of the major themes of country music songs, this one fits right in. Remember they were still together when he recorded this song, but it would prove to be prophetic.

He also hit number one in 1974 with "The Door". George must have known that the end was near, for this is another "you're leaving" song. He sings about all of the sounds that have bothered him over his life, but the worse is the lonely sound of the closing of the door (as she leaves).

The next song he recorded was "These Days (I Barely Get By)," which was co-written by Tammy. It reached number ten on the charts, but it was a hollow victory. Two days later, Tammy walked out. This time she filed for divorce, she did not retract it and a year later they split for good. The divorce became final on March 13, 1975. If you've ever had an addiction, you know what happens when adversity comes into your life. You retreat into the bottle or the pills or whatever it is. It doesn't matter that those are what caused the adversity in the first place. You sink even lower into your habit. Keep in mind that I'm not a professional, these are just my observations.

I can't leave the marriage of George and Tammy without mentioning their daughter. Tamala Georgette Jones was born to the couple in 1970. She began singing with her mom and dad as early as three years old. She became a backup singer for her mom. Later, she wrote songs for her father and they sang a few duets together. She even went on tour with George a couple of times. Today, she is still an active country singer.

George had now lost three wives, two of which were a direct result of his drinking and drug abuse. He added cocaine to his repertoire and things went from bad to worse. The last five years of the Seventies, he only hit the Top 10 twice as a solo artist with "These Days (I Barely Get By)" (#10) in 1975 and "Her Name Is" (#3) in 1976. His health suffered and he began to miss concerts. He became notorious for his drunken rampages. He would disappear for days at a time. In 1979 alone, he missed 54 shows and picked up a new nickname, "No-Show Jones". Someone said that buying a ticket to a Jones concert was like buying a lottery ticket. Would it pay off or not, no one knew.

George says there were promoters that took advantage of his "no-show" reputation. They would advertise that he was coming to town without even telling George or expecting him to show up. Then they would sell liquor at the concert and tell the people he would be right out. By the time, they got to the point where they had to admit that he wasn't coming, the crowd was too drunk to care and few actually asked for their money back. That was a pretty good racket; George got the blame just based on his reputation.

"GOLDEN RING"

He and Tammy, although divorced, continued to record together. In 1976, they recorded what is probably their signature song together, "Golden Ring". The song was their second number one as a duo. It was written by Bobby Braddock, a long time writer of country music. The song was inspired by a television show which was broadcast in the early Seventies. The show was about the life of a handgun. It showed how the gun had changed hands over the years, owned by a police officer and by a hunter and finally by a father with a young son. And it showed the consequences for each of owning the handgun.

Bobby decided to write a song about a wedding ring and the life of the ring. Listen to the song by George and Tammy as they portray the life of the ring. It starts out in a pawn shop in Chicago. A young couple, deeply in love, come in and buys the ring. It's not much, but it's all they can afford. They are married and start their life. The song doesn't say what happened; only that they eventually break up and the ring ends up back in the pawn shop where the song started.

George and Tammy recorded the song in 1976, but didn't sing it publically until two years later when they appeared on a television show "Pop Goes the Country". There is a video of the appearance and as George sings the words that the boy sings in the song, "I Don't Love You Anymore", he looks right at Tammy and Tammy looks down at the floor. It's probably just me, but it looks to me like he does still love her.

They followed up "Golden Ring" with another one later in 1976. "Near You" spent two weeks at number one. When they performed the song on "Pop Goes the Country", George said "Tammy, after seven years of marriage" and Tammy adds, "and two years of divorce", he then concludes with, "it's still wonderful to be near you".

Tammy nods and says thank you. You can't tell me they didn't still have feelings for each other.

"Near You" is an old standard from 1947 when Francis Craig and his orchestra spent seventeen weeks at number one with the song. The vocals were done by Bob Lamm and the song eventually became the theme song of the Milton Berle Show in the Fifties.

In 1978, he hit number six with a collaboration with James Taylor called "Bartender's Blues". Taylor also wrote the song. To my knowledge, this is the only time he worked with James Taylor. He also got together with Johnny Paycheck who had started out in the Sixties by playing in several different bands, including George's. In 1977 Paycheck recorded the iconic "Take This Job and Shove It" which was a number one song. He and George recorded the old Chuck Berry classic "Maybelline" in the traditional manner and it reached number seven on the charts. They followed that up with "You Can Have Her" which is also a Fifties song originally done by Roy Hamilton. Both songs come from an album called "Double Trouble" and are available on Amazon in CD form. I notice as of this writing someone is asking $89.99 for a new copy, so this looks like it could be pretty valuable today.

His success with duets motivated Epic records to release an album of just duets called "My Very Special Guests". The first copy that came out in 1979 had ten songs and featured guests like Waylon Jennings, Tammy Wynette and Emmy Lou Harris. But if you want to buy this album, hunt down the release that came out in 2005 in which thirty-one more songs are added and it became a double CD album. This includes everyone who was anyone in country (and a couple from pop) and is well worth the money.

"HE STOPPED LOVING HER TODAY"

Despite failing health, George began to make a real comeback in 1980. It started with another duet with Tammy. I am happy that they remained close enough that they could still record together. Tammy could have walked away and never looked back. The song "Two Story House" (#2) in 1980 seemed like another lament on their marriage which, by this time had been over for six years. The song explains that they live in a two story house. I have my story and she has hers, but there's no love here. Kind of a sad song.

Writer Bobby Braddock and his associate Curly Putman wrote what was to become one of the greatest country songs of all time. They pitched "He Stopped Loving Her Today" to George and he hated it. He thought it was too long, too sad, too depressing. But, heck, that's the way life is sometimes.

The song is about a man who has loved a woman his entire life, but apparently she did not return his love. Finally, the man has died and his friends realize that he has finally stopped loving her. She did come to his funeral, so maybe she had more feelings for him than he knew.

George was in bad shape during the recording of the song. From the first time they tried to get it recorded until he finally finished the recitation or the speaking part in the song was eighteen months. When it was finally done, George walked out of the studio and said "Nobody'll buy that morbid son of a bitch".

But people did buy it. The song only spent one week at number one, but it is responsible for bringing George back into the spotlight and gave a much needed boost to his career. George would win the Grammy that year for Best Male Country Vocal Performance. It was also named Single of the Year and Song of the Year for 1980 by the Academy of Country Music as well as the Song of the Year for both

1980 and 1981 by the Country Music Association. You don't get any better than that.

He followed that up with "I'm Not Ready Yet", a number two song in 1980. George was firing on all cylinders again; at least some of the time. Between 1981 and 1983, George had eight Top 10 songs, some solo and some with a little help from his friends. They include "If Drinkin' Don't Kill Me (Her Memory Will)" (#8), "Still Doin' Time" which was George's eighth number one as a solo artist. Then the Oak Ridge Boys joined him on "Same Ole Me" (#5) in 1982.

Going back to the duet formula that had worked so well before; George got together with Merle Haggard for an album ("A Taste of Yesterday's Wine") which contained two hits. "Yesterday's Wine" became another number one in his career. The song had originally been done by Willie Nelson back in 1971, but had not made the Top 40. Merle also helped him on "C.C.Waterback" (#10) in 1982 which is essentially about the evils (or maybe I should say the joys) of drinking. It's a fun song with a Dixieland flavor that makes you forget about the aching head and just enjoy the music.

His next big hit was also his ninth number one solo song and probably my second most favorite George Jones. "I Always Get Lucky With You" spent one week at number one and a total of thirteen weeks on the charts. Unlike so many other songs he recorded, this song, to me, at least, feels very positive and uplifting. He sings that he's had good luck and bad luck and no luck at all, but he always gets lucky with his lady that he singing to. I know just how he feels. And, we talk today about "Getting lucky" as a euphemism for sex, but I don't think George is singing about sex. I believe he is just singing the praises of the lady he is in love with. "I Always Get Lucky With You" would be his last number one song, not quite the end of a career, but an end to hitting the top.

MARRIAGE NUMBER FOUR

Actually things were about to turnaround for George. Maybe the lady he was singing about was Nancy Sepulvado. George met Nancy while touring for his hit "He Stopped Loving Her Today". Nancy says she knew what she was getting into by associating with him and then marrying him. She says she could see the good inside of him and felt he could change. Well he did. He married Nancy on March 4, 1983 in Woodville, Texas. She would become his manager and is directly responsible for cleaning up George Jones.

George was a mess when they got married. He had reached a point when he was so sick that the doctors told him he only had two or three days to live. He had to quit drinking or he would die. It was that simple. With Nancy's help, almost immediately after they got married, George entered detox treatment and by the end of 1983, he claimed he was completely rehabilitated. He and Nancy would remain married until his death in 2013.

A song which came out in late 1983 was "Tennessee Whiskey" which peaked at number two. The song, written by Dean Dillon and Linda Hargrove, was originally done by David Allan Coe, but didn't chart. George gave it the Jones touch and it was a hit. This was five months after "I Always Get Lucky With You" and this was the time George was in rehab. The song sounds like a tribute to Nancy as it discusses how he used to spend his time in the bar drinking and now he gets stoned on her love. "You're as smooth as Tennessee Whiskey" is talking about Nancy, I believe.

As bad as things were before, they were just the opposite now. "No Show Jones" disappeared and instead became "Old Reliable". He was everywhere he was supposed to be. He never missed a concert and, more importantly, except for a few brief falls off the wagon, he remained sober and clean. Life was good again and he had Nancy to thank for it. You can't help but wonder if he had been able to do this while he was married to Tammy Wynette, they might have stayed together.

A song I have to mention is "The One I Loved Back Then (The Corvette Song)" which hit number three in 1985. It's the story of a man who drives up to a Kwik-Mart for some beer and cigarettes and the old man behind the counter is admiring the man's car, a Corvette. He says I had one just like it back in '63. The cool thing about this song is that hardly anyone remembers the title of the song. Everyone know it as "Hotter Than a $2 Pistol". Those words followed George for the rest of his life. Even at his funeral, some were talking about how George was "hotter than a $2 pistol".

Another cute song from George was "Who's Gonna Fill Their Shoes". The song comes from an album by the same name and has become one of George's most famous songs. In 1985, a number of great country singers had passed away and this song honors them by asking who will fill the shoes of these great artists. The song is really about how unique these performers are and how hard it will be to replace them. He talks about some who were still alive in 1985 and are still alive today, like Jerry Lee Lewis and Willie Nelson, but most of the names are of those who have left us, Hank Williams, Conway Twitty, Waylon Jennings and many more. Songs like this always make me tear up a little when I realize just what we have lost. But, thank goodness, their music is still here to listen to. They will never be truly gone.

In 1988, he recorded another song which is pure George Jones. "I'm a One Woman Man" was originally done in 1956 by the late Johnny Horton. He reached number seven on the charts. George covered it in 1988 and beat Horton by two, peaking at number five. The song is unique because of the subject matter. George was on his fourth wife by this time, so the title is kind of tongue-in-cheek, but I particularly like the changes in voice during the song. George's voice starts out high pitched as most George Jones songs are and then he goes way low to a bass register. It produces a really cool effect. If you haven't heard it lately, go find it on YouTube and listen to it.

THE END OF TRADITIONAL COUNTRY

While traditional country didn't go away completely, it changed greatly in the Nineties. We were into the era of Garth Brooks and Dwight Yokum and Tim McGraw. The sound of country was changing and George just couldn't make the change. George tried, but his style of music was so ingrained into him that he just couldn't do it. He did get together with Randy Travis for a duet in 1990 called "A Few Ole Country Boys". The song celebrates that there are still a few old country boys around. Travis was the perfect partner to sing this song as he was one who managed to straddle the line between old country and new country. The song peaked at number five on the charts.

But that song would be George's last Top 10 song of his career. He would still chart and actually got as high as fourteen (with Patti Loveless in "You Don't Seem to Miss Me"), but that was the best he was able to do for the rest of his career. He became relegated to the position of "Living Legend". Everyone knew him and loved his music. But no one was buying it anymore.

In 1991, George changed labels again, this time signing with MCA. The President of MCA said the event was like signing Elvis. Of course, George was in decline by this time, so I think he was being overly optimistic. .

A couple standouts in the last ten years or so which George recorded for MCA are "I Don't Need Your Rockin' Chair" which didn't do that well on the charts, (only peaking at number thirty four) but everybody knows it's about George Jones when they hear it and it's still a great song. George is making fun of the fact that he's getting old and while the world may be trying to put him out to pasture, he's not ready to go just yet.

You can see the all-star performance of this song on YouTube. To show how much the country community loved George Jones, the song features ten of the biggest names in Country Music singing backup for George. They are Mark Chesnutt, Garth Brooks, Travis Tritt, Joe Diffee, Alan Jackson, Pam Tillis, T Graham Browne, Patty Loveless and Clint Black. They are all showing their love for George.

A song I rather liked because MTV was playing the video at the time was "High Tech Redneck" (#24) in 1993. The song is all about the wonders of technology in 1993. "Mayberry meets Star Trek". The words were so technical sounding in 1993. Today, it sounds very old fashioned.

George got back together with Tammy Wynette one last time in 1995 to record the album "One" which contained the single by the same name. This was the first time they had sung together in twenty years. They even toured together to promote the album. The album reached number twelve on the charts which was a good effort, but the careers of both performers were fading. I think it's wonderful that George and Tammy were able to put their differences aside in those later years and actually become friends. In the end, there was peace between them.

TAMMY PASSES AWAY

Because Tammy had such an important part of George Jones' life, I have to mention her death. Tammy had become addicted herself, to pain killers. She had had years of medical problems, more than fifteen surgeries and numerous trips to the hospital. Along the way, she had become addicted to pain killers and this further affected her health. On April 9, 1998, she fell asleep on her couch in her living room and passed away in her sleep.

Tammy was survived by her husband George Richey, four daughters and eight granddaughters. She performed right up until her death and, in fact, had several shows planned in advance which would have to be cancelled. She was placed in a crypt at Woodlawn Memorial Cemetery in Nashville, Tennessee. A memorial service was held for her at the Ryman Theater which is famous as the former home of the Grand Ole Opry until 1974. It is still used today for special occasions.

In a weird twist of events, three of her daughters claimed that George Richey had had something to do with her death. They convinced the authorities to exhume the body and do another autopsy. But this one showed that she had died of a cardiac arrhythmia which means an irregular heartbeat. Whether it was brought on by the medication she was taking, we will probably never know. At any rate George Richey was exonerated from any wrong doing in her death and Tammy was laid to rest again. In 2012, the name over the grave was changed from Tammy Wynette to Virginia W Richardson which was her legal name at time of death.

THE DECLINING YEARS

In the summer of 1994, George started feeling tired over the least bit of exertion. Nancy wanted him to go to a doctor, but he refused. He began to get upset over little things and started fights for no reason. If this was 1955, then you could explain it away as George just being George, but George had changed over the years. He was now sixty two and clean and sober and there was no reason for the behavior.

Nancy finally convinced him to see a doctor and they found out he had an irregular heartbeat. They did further tests and found that of the four arteries entering his heart, one was 100% blocked, another 95% blocked and a third 50% blocked. He was just days away from a fatal heart attack. George, of course, didn't want to have surgery. He asked what would happen if he didn't. The doctor said, you'll be dead in three or four days. So a triple bypass was done on September 12, 1994, George's sixty third birthday.

George says many of the great stars of Country Music came to see him at the hospital. During the surgery, they gathered in the waiting room and sang songs together. Several called every hour to see how he was doing. Then the mail started pouring in; letters of concern. Nancy stopped counting at 10,000.

In 1997, George decided to tell the world the real story of his life (at least the way he remembered it). "I Lived to Tell It All" was published and is still available to this day. He then recorded an album with the same name which peaked at number 26.

For a couple of years, George had his own show on the then TNN (The Nashville Network). Called The George Jones Show, the show was a typical country variety show, but George featured all the greats in Country Music in the late Nineties. You can watch full episodes on YouTube and this is as close as you can get to seeing a live George

Jones Concert. TNN went through a couple changes over the years and today is Spike TV.

In 1999 George recorded a song which didn't do that well on the charts, but, I think, spoke to his heart as he repented for the damage he had done throughout his life. The song, "Choices" is from the album "Cold Hard Truth". The song was written by Mike Curtis and Billy Yates. Yates recorded the song first, but it didn't do anything. George sings "I'm living and dying by the choices I've made". Don't we all. The single only reached number thirty on the charts, but the album "Cold Hard Truth" peaked at number five, the first Top 10 album he had had since 1986.

An interesting story is associated with this song. At the Country Music Awards (CMA) Awards in 1999, George was scheduled to sing "Choices" live, but the show was running long and the producers asked him if he could shorten it some. George said, he couldn't do that and so elected to stay home and didn't attend the award show. The other performers had heard about this and during Alan Jackson's set, he sang his hit "Pop-a-Top" which was a big hit that year. About 2 minutes into the song. Jackson stops and then he and the band launch into a 30 second excerpt from "Choices". Everyone in the room knew exactly what was going on and he got a standing ovation. Everyone loved George.

Also that year (1999), while recording "Cold Hard Truth", George fell off the wagon and drove his SUV into a concrete bridge and went to the hospital with damaged lungs and liver. It took the EMT's two hours to free him from the car. The doctors found he had a collapsed lung, a torn liver and various other internal injuries. He was in Intensive Care for eleven days and on a ventilator to help him breathe much of that time. We came very close to losing him, then, but he recovered, finished the album and went back on tour. He got a ticket for DUI that night and it had the effect of sobering up George for good. To my knowledge, he never drank to excess again.

His last album was "Burn Your Playhouse Down – The Unreleased Duets", released in 2008. While none of this was new material, it had never been heard by the public before. The album contained left over songs from previous duet albums and featured people like Dolly Parton and his daughter, Georgette Jones. It even included a couple rock stars like Leon Russell and Mark Knopfler.

THE LAST FEW YEARS

His last single to hit the charts was "Beer Run" (B-double E-double R You In), a duet with Garth Brooks in 2001. It reached number twenty four and was the 165th single that he charted in his lifetime.

On April 18, 2013, George was admitted to Vanderbilt University Medical Center in Nashville, Tennessee with a high fever and irregular blood pressure. The doctors did what they could, but on April 26, 2013, George passed away. His years of abuse finally caught up with him. He was 81 years old. The cause of death was officially listed as "Hypoxic Respiratory Failure" which means the lungs couldn't pump enough oxygen to sustain the body. George just suffocated.

TMZ reported that Alan Jackson said "Well, heaven better get ready for some great country music."

A few days later, on May 2, 2013, a memorial was held at the Grand Ole Opry in Nashville. It was attended by the famous from country music and the otherwise famous. Barbara Bush, former first lady gave a eulogy, as did news personality Bob Schieffer of CBS News. Bill Haslam, the governor of Tennessee spoke and a whole long list of performers sang their tributes to George by singing some of his more famous songs. I have the entire thing on my DVR and it's been almost two months and I can't bring myself to erase it.

The week after George's death, "He Stopped Loving Her Today" re-entered the Country charts at number 21.

On his Facebook page, Brad Paisley had this to say about George:

"George Jones' life is an example of so many wonderful things; how someone's God-given gifts can make this a richer, better place. How one human being can overcome adversity, addiction, and life threatening obstacles time and time again. That it is not the stumble

or fall that counts, but the willingness to stand again. How a keen sense of humor and a twinkle in a person's eye can still prevail even after all of life's hard knocks. How mistakes, missteps, and bad choices are not the end of the world if a person chooses to turn them into something good. And George's life is above all the strongest example of how the love of a great woman can get a man through anything. All of this made its way beautifully into every note of the greatest voice country music will ever know and one of the greatest friends you could ever have. We miss you already, George."

I use that without his permission, so I hope he doesn't mind. It says everything I would like to say about George Jones. Rest in peace, George, no one will ever fill your shoes.

LEGACY OF GEORGE JONES

Frank Sinatra (yes, *that* Frank Sinatra) once remarked that George Jones was "the second greatest singer in America" I wonder who he considered number one.

George had 165 hits on the Country charts over his career, both as a solo artist and with other artists. A large number of them were duets. He is one of only a handful of artists who have had a hit in every decade since the Fifties, up to and including 2000-2010. That is six consecutive decades.

George was made a member of the Grand Ole Opry in 1956 and remained a member throughout his life.

The list of George Jones awards is long, so I will just mention a few.

He was voted Most Promising New Country Vocalist in 1956. He was inducted into the Country Music Hall of Fame in 1992.

In 2008, President George Bush presided over the Kennedy Center Honors as George was inducted. Performers who were there to pay tribute to George were Brad Paisley, Randy Travis, Alan Taylor and Garth Brooks. At the end of Garth Brooks' set, he took off his hat and bowed to George as honoree. He said "Here's to the greatest voice to ever sing country music". Amen.

In 2012, he was presented with a Grammy Lifetime Achievement Award. His friend Merle Haggard presented it to him.

George was Billboard's Male Vocalist of the year in 1962 and 1963.

Let's just summarize his Grammy awards. In 1980, he won the Grammy for Best Male Country Vocal Performance for "He Stopped Loving Her Today", Hall of Fame Award for "She Thinks I Still Care" in 1996, Grammy for Best Male Country Vocal Performance for "Choices" in 1999 and Grammy Hall of Fame Award for "He Stopped Loving Her Today" in 2007.

He won CMA awards in 1980, 1981, 1986, 1993, 1998, 2001 and 2003.

In 2002, he received the U.S. National Medal of Arts from the National Endowment for the Arts.

The city of Corpus Christi, Texas gave him the key to the city in 2007.

And, last but not least, in 2010, he was inducted into the Texas Country Music Hall of Fame.

AFTERWORD

George enjoyed success right up until he died. He never compromised on what he felt was true country music. He would often sing with other performers, even the new generation like Garth Brooks, but when you heard George sing, you knew it was him. No one else has that distinctive voice.

I will always remember the evening in Nevada when my wife and I sat in the audience and listened to him sing. He was in his mid-Seventies then, but his voice was strong and as clear as ever. When he started into "He Stopped Loving Her Today", he just sang the opening line "He said I'll love you 'til I die" and the audience were on its feet roaring and clapping. It was magical. George just smiled and went on with the song.

As of this writing, George has been gone about 2 months, now. It's hard to say I miss him. He hadn't really been a part of the country music scene for a while, so it just seems like he's away, retired, enjoying life. I play a lot of the music of the artist when I prepare these little books and I always choke up on certain songs, especially when the artist is gone and I know I will never hear it live again.

George Jones will always live in my heart and I hope, if you're a country fan that you feel the same way, too.

You can contact me at www.number1project.com where I occasionally blog about things that interest me in the music world (mostly, the twentieth century). Go find it and read it and leave me a comment. I also have a Facebook fan page called "Legends of Rock & Roll". "Like" me and comment there, too. If you love the music as much as I do, you'll enjoy the trip. Thanks for reading.

I hope you have enjoyed this book as much as I have enjoyed writing it for you.

If you have liked what you read, will you please do me a favor and leave a review of "George Jones". Thank you.

SELECTED DISCOGRAPHY

Studio Albums

1957 Grand Ole Opry's New Star

1958 Hillbilly Hit Parade

1958 Long Live King George

1959 Country Church Time

1959 White Lightning and Other Favorites

1960 George Jones Salutes Hank Williams

1962 Sings Country and Western Hits

1962 Songs from the Heart

1962 George Jones Sings Bob Wills

1962 Homecoming in Heaven

1962 My Favorites of Hank Williams

1963 I Wish Tonight Would Never End

1964 Blue and Lonesome

1964 Heartaches and Tears

1964 George Jones Sings Like The Dickens!

1964 I Get Lonely in a Hurry

1965 The Race Is On

1965 Mr. Country & Western Music

1965 New Country Hits

1965 Old Brush Arbors

1965 Trouble in Mind

1966 Country Heart

1966 Love Bug

1966 I'm a People

1966 We Found Heaven Right Here on Earth at "4033"

1967 Walk Through This World with Me

1968 Sings the Songs of Dallas Frazier

1968 If My Heart Had Windows

1968 The George Jones Story

1969 My Country

1969 I'll Share My World with You

1969 Where Grass Won't Grow

1970 Will You Visit Me on Sunday?

1971 George Jones with Love

1971 George Jones Sings the Great Songs of Leon Payne

1972 George Jones (We Can Make It)

1972 A Picture of Me (Without You)

1973 Nothing Ever Hurt Me (Half as Bad as Losing You)

1973 In a Gospel Way

1974 George Jones Sings His Songs

1974 The Grand Tour

1975 Memories of Us

1976 The Battle

1976 Alone Again

1977 I Wanta Sing

1978 Bartender's Blues

1980 I Am What I Am

1981 Still the Same Ole Me

1983 Shine On

1983 Jones Country

1984 You've Still Got a Place in My Heart

1984 Ladies' Choice

1985 Who's Gonna Fill Their Shoes

1986 Wine Colored Roses

1987 Too Wild Too Long

1989 One Woman Man

1990 You Oughta Be Here with Me

1991 Friends in High Places

1991 And Along Came Jones

1992 Walls Can Fall

1993 High-Tech Redneck

1996 I Lived to Tell It All

1998 It Don't Get Any Better Than This

1999 Cold Hard Truth

2001 The Rock: Stone Cold Country 2001

2003 The Gospel Collection

2005 Hits I Missed...And One I Didn't

2008 Burn Your Playhouse Down - The Unreleased Duets

Collaborative albums

1963 What's in Our Hearts (with Melba Montgomery)

1964 A King & Two Queens (with Melba Montgomery and Judy Lynn)

1964 Bluegrass Hootenanny (with Melba Montgomery)

1965 Famous Country Duets (with Gene Pitney and Melba Montgomery)

1965 George Jones and Gene Pitney: For the First Time! Two Great Singers (with Gene Pitney)

1965 George Jones and Gene Pitney (Recorded in Nashville) (with Gene Pitney)

1966 It's Country Time Again! (with Gene Pitney)

1966 Close Together (As You and Me) (with Melba Montgomery)

1967 Let's Get Together (with Melba Montgomery)

1979 My Very Special Guests

1980 Double Trouble (with Johnny Paycheck)

1982 A Taste of Yesterday's Wine (with Merle Haggard)

1987 Walking the Line (with Merle Haggard and Willie Nelson)

1994 Bradley Barn Sessions

2006 God's Country: George Jones and Friends

2006 Kicking Out the Footlights...Again (with Merle Haggard)

Studio Albums with Tammy Wynette

1971 We Go Together

1972 Me and the First Lady

1972 We Love to Sing About Jesus

1973 Let's Build a World Together

1973 We're Gonna Hold On

1975 George & Tammy & Tina (with Tina Byrd)

1976 Golden Ring

1980 Together Again

1995 One

<u>*Singles*</u>

1954 "No Money in This Deal"

1954 "Play It Cool, Man"

1954 "Let Him Know"

1954 "You All Goodnight"

1955 "Why Baby Why"

1956 "What Am I Worth"

1956 "You Gotta Be My Baby"

1956 "Just One More"

1957 "Yearning" (with Jeanette Hicks)

1957 "Don't Stop the Music"

1957 "Too Much Water"

1958 "Color of the Blues"

1958 "Treasure of Love"

1959 "White Lightning"

1959 "Who Shot Sam"

1959 "Money to Burn"

1960 "Accidentally on Purpose"

1960 "Out of Control"

1960 "Window Up Above"

1961 "Family Bible"

1961 "Tender Years"

1962 "Aching, Breaking Heart"

1962 "She Thinks I Still Care"

1962 "Open Pit Mine"

1962 "A Girl I Used to Know"

1963 "Not What I Had in Mind"

1963 "You Comb Her Hair"

1964 "Your Heart Turned Left (And I Was on the Right)"

1964 "Where Does a Little Tear Come From"

1964 "The Race Is On"

1965 "Least of All"

1965 "Love Bug"

1965 "Take Me"

1966 "I'm a People"

1966 "Old Brush Arbors"

1966 "Four-O-Thirty-Three"

1967 "Walk Through This World with Me"

1967 "I Can't Get There from Here"

1967 "If My Heart Had Windows"

1968 "Say It's Not You"

1968 "Small Time Laboring Man"

1968 "As Long as I Live"

1968 "Milwaukee, Here I Come" <small>(with Brenda Carter)</small>

1968 "When the Grass Grows Over Me'"

1969 "I'll Share My World with You"

1969 "If Not for You"

1969 "She's Mine"

1970 "Where Grass Won't Grow"

1970 "Tell Me My Lying Eyes Are Wrong"

1970 "A Good Year for the Roses"

1971 "Sometimes You Just Can't Win"

1971 "Right Won't Touch a Hand"

1971 "I'll Follow You (Up to Our Cloud)"

1972 "We Can Make It"

1972 "Loving You Could Never Be Better"

1972 "A Picture of Me (Without You)"

1973 "What My Woman Can't Do"

1973 "Nothing Ever Hurt Me (Half as Bad as Losing You)"

1973 "Once You've Had the Best"

1974 "The Grand Tour"

1974 "The Door"

1974 "These Days (I Barely Get By)"

1975 "Memories of Us"

1976 "The Battle"

1976 "You Always Look Your Best (Here in My Arms)"

1976 "Her Name Is"

1977 "Old King Kong"

1977 "If I Could Put Them All Together (I'd Have You)"

1978 "Bartender's Blues"

1978 "I'll Just Take It Out in Love"

1979 "Someday My Day Will Come"

1980 "He Stopped Loving Her Today"

1980 "I'm Not Ready Yet"

1981 "If Drinkin' Don't Kill Me (Her Memory Will)"

1981 "Still Doin' Time"

1982 "Same Ole Me" (with The Oak Ridge Boys)

1983 "Shine On (Shine All Your Sweet Love on Me)"

1983 "I Always Get Lucky with You"

1983 "Tennessee Whiskey"

1984 "You've Still Got a Place in My Heart"

1984 "She's My Rock"

1984 "Hallelujah, I Love You So" (with Brenda Lee)

1984 "Size Seven Round (Made of Gold)" (with Lacy J. Dalton)

1985 "Who's Gonna Fill Their Shoes"

1985 "The One I Loved Back Then (The Corvette Song)"

1986 "Somebody Wants Me Out of the Way"

1986 "Wine Colored Roses"

1987 "The Right Left Hand"

1987 "I Turn to You"

1987 "The Bird"

1988 "I'm a Survivor"

1988 "The Old Man No One Loves"

1988 "If I Could Bottle This Up" (with Shelby Lynne)

1988 "(I'm a) One Woman Man"

1989 "The King Is Gone (So Are You)"

1989 "Writing on the Wall"

1989 "Radio Lover"

1990 "Hell Stays Open (All Night Long)"

1990 "Six Foot Deep Six Foot Down"

1991 "All Fall Down" (with Emmylou Harris)

1991 "You Couldn't Get the Picture"

1992 "She Loved a Lot in Her Time"

1992 "Honky Tonk Myself to Death"

1992 "I Don't Need Your Rockin' Chair"

1993 "Wrong's What I Do Best"

1993 "Walls Can Fall"

1993 "High-Tech Redneck"

1994 "Never Bit a Bullet Like This" (with Sammy Kershaw)

1994 "A Good Year for the Roses" (with Alan Jackson)

1996 "Honky Tonk Song"

1996 "Billy B. Bad"

1998 "Wild Irish Rose"

1998 "No Future in Our Past"

1999 "Choices"

1999 "The Cold Hard Truth"

2000 "Sinners and Saints"

2001 "The Man He Was"

2001 "Beer Run (B Double E Double Are You In?)" (with Garth Brooks)

2002 "50,000 Names"

2005 "The Blues Man" (with Dolly Parton)

2006 "Funny How Time Slips Away"

2006 "God's Country"

2008 "You and Me and Time" (with Georgette Jones)

Single Collaborations

1961 "Did I Ever Tell You" (with Margie Singleton)

1962 "Waltz of the Angels" (with Margie Singleton)

1963 "We Must Have Been Out of Our Minds" (with Melba Montgomery)

1963 "Let's Invite Them Over" (with Melba Montgomery)

1964 "Please Be My Love" (with Melba Montgomery)

1964 "Multiply the Heartaches" (with Melba Montgomery)

1965 "Things Have Gone to Pieces" (with Gene Pitney)

1965 "I've Got Five Dollars and It's Saturday Night" (with Gene Pitney)

1965 "Louisiana Man" (with Gene Pitney)

1965 "Big Job" (with Gene Pitney)

1966 "That's All It Took" (with Melba Montgomery)

1966 "Close Together (As You and Me)" (with Melba Montgomery)

1967 "Party Pickin" (with Melba Montgomery)

1974 "The Telephone Call" (with stepdaughter Tina Byrd)

1978 "Maybellene" (with Johnny Paycheck)

1979 "You Can Have Her" (with Johnny Paycheck)

1980 "When You're Ugly Like Us (You Just Naturally Got to Be Cool)" (with Johnny Paycheck)

1980 "You Better Move On" (with Johnny Paycheck)

1982 "Yesterday's Wine" (with Merle Haggard)

1982 "C.C. Waterback" (with Merle Haggard)

Single Collaborations with Tammy Wynette

1971 "Take Me"

1972 "The Ceremony"

1972 "Old Fashioned Singing"

1973 "Let's Build a World Together"

1973 "We're Gonna Hold On"

1974 "(We're Not) the Jet Set"

1974 "We Loved It Away"

1975 "God's Gonna Get'cha (For That)"

1976 "Golden Ring"

1976 "Near You"

1977 "Southern California"

1980 "Two Story House"

1980 "A Pair of Old Sneakers"

1995 "One"

ABOUT THE AUTHOR

James Hoag has always been a big fan of Rock & Roll. Most people graduate from high school and then proceed to "grow up" and go on to more adult types of music. James got stuck at about age 18 and has been an avid fan of popular music ever since. His favorite music is from the Fifties, the origin of Rock & Roll and which was the era in which James grew up. But he likes almost all types of popular music including country music.

In 1980, he became friends with a man who introduced him to Country Music and he has been a strong fan of that genre of music ever since.

After working his entire life as a computer programmer, he is now retired, and he decided to share his love of the music and of the performers by writing books that discuss the life and music of the various people who have meant so much to him over the years.

He calls each book a "love letter" to the stars that have enriched our lives so much. These people are truly Legends.

Printed in Poland
by Amazon Fulfillment
Poland Sp. z o.o., Wrocław